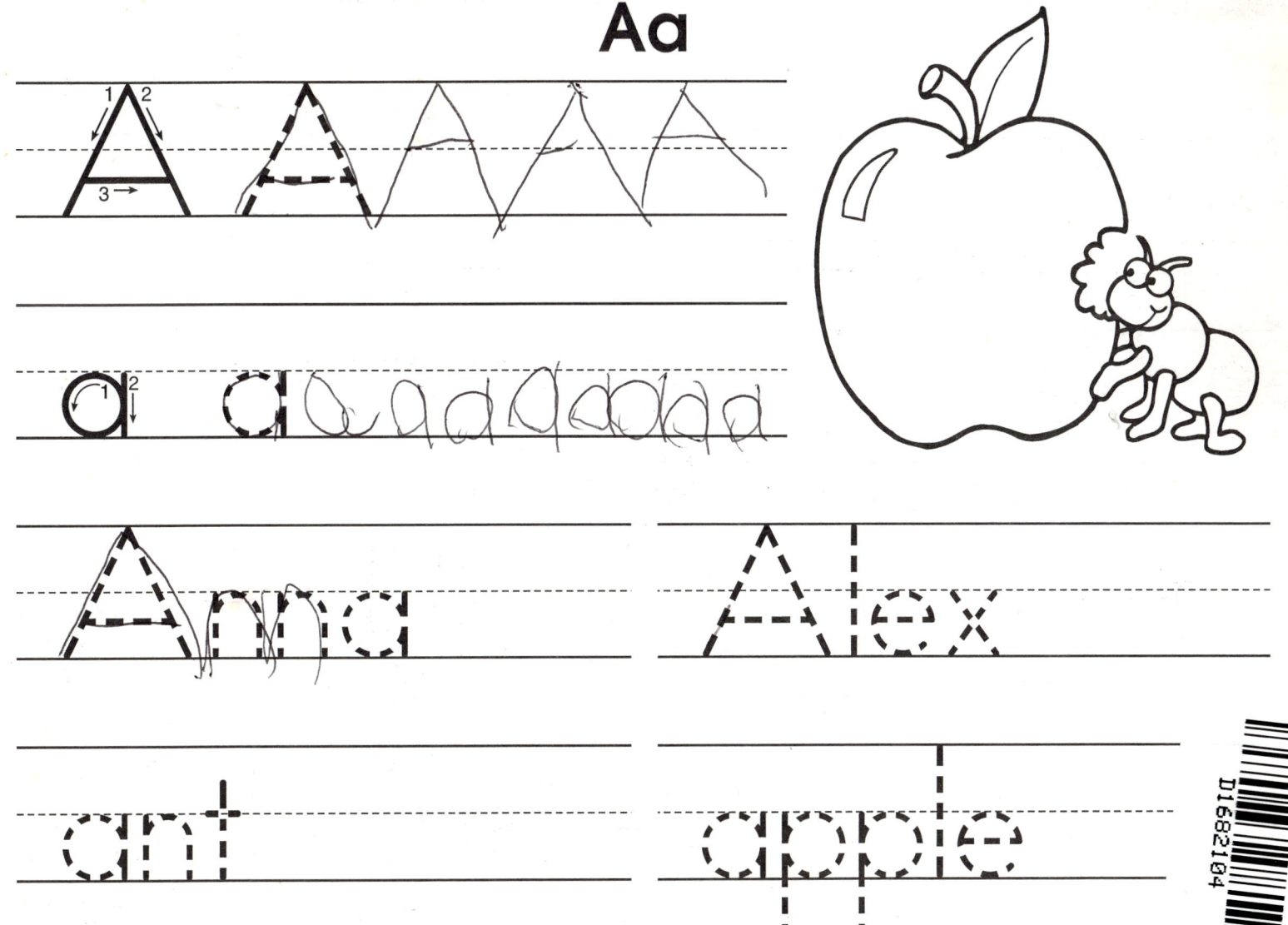

Bb

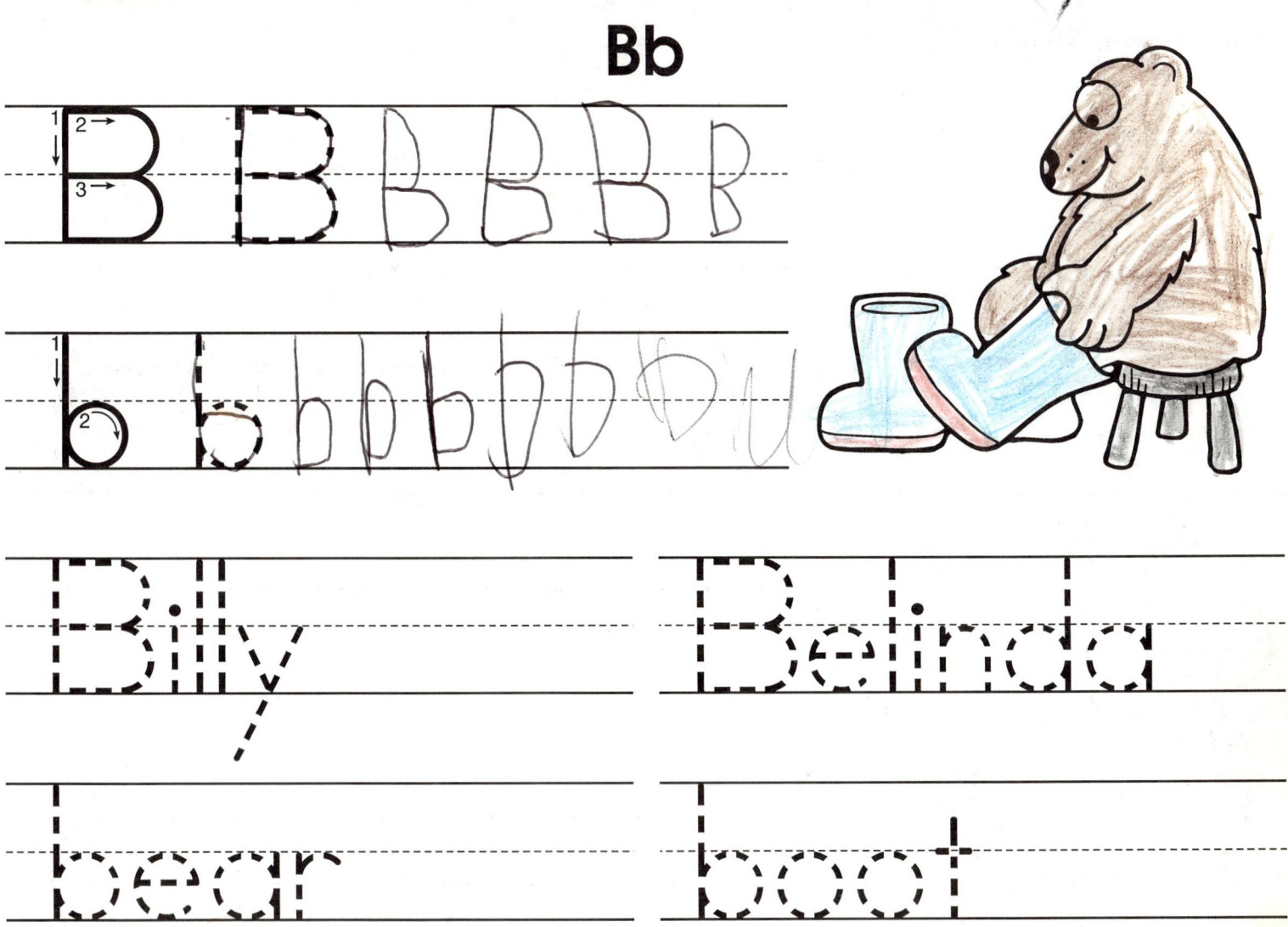

Cc

Carrie Chris

camel cake

Dd

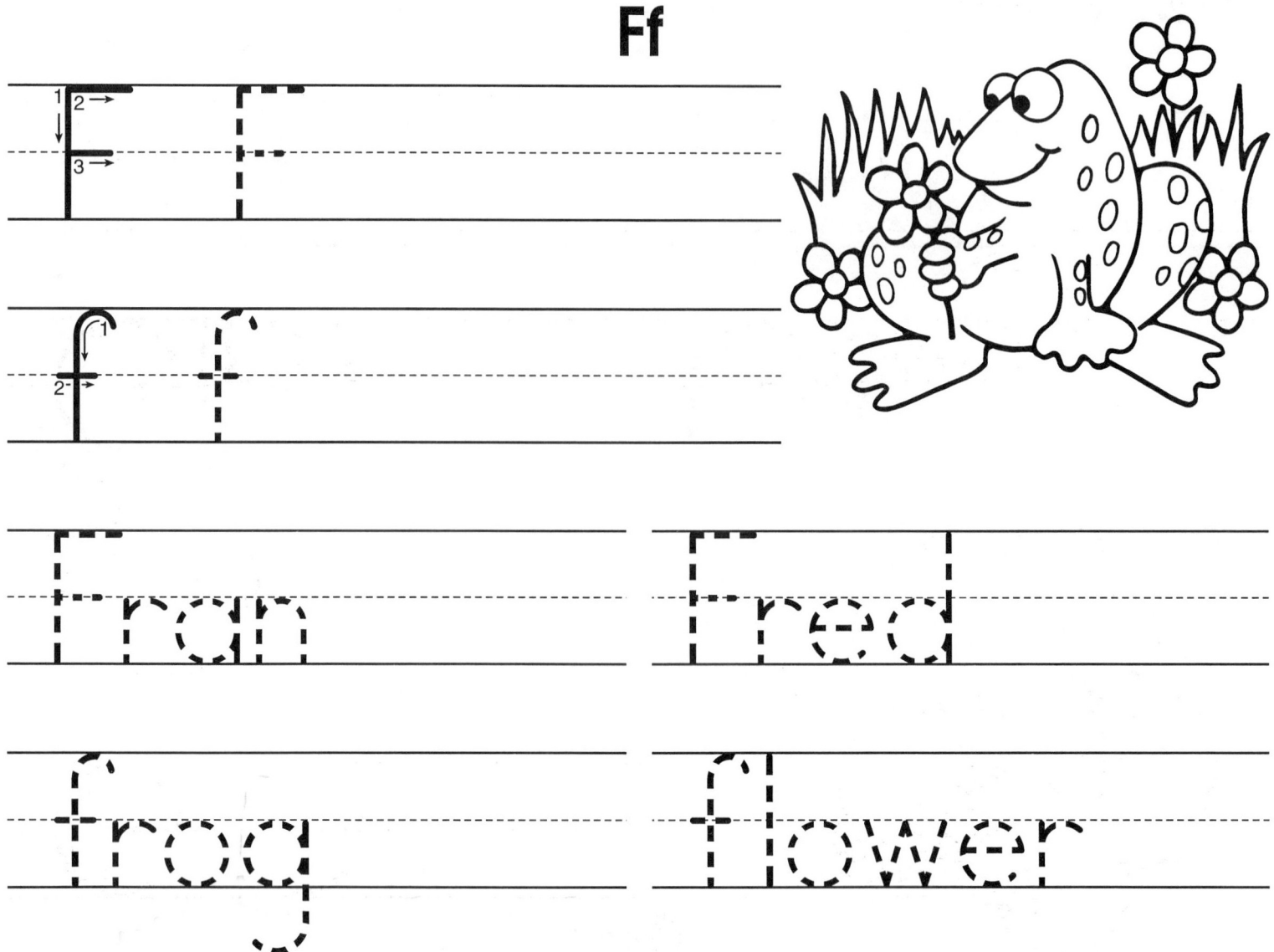

Hh

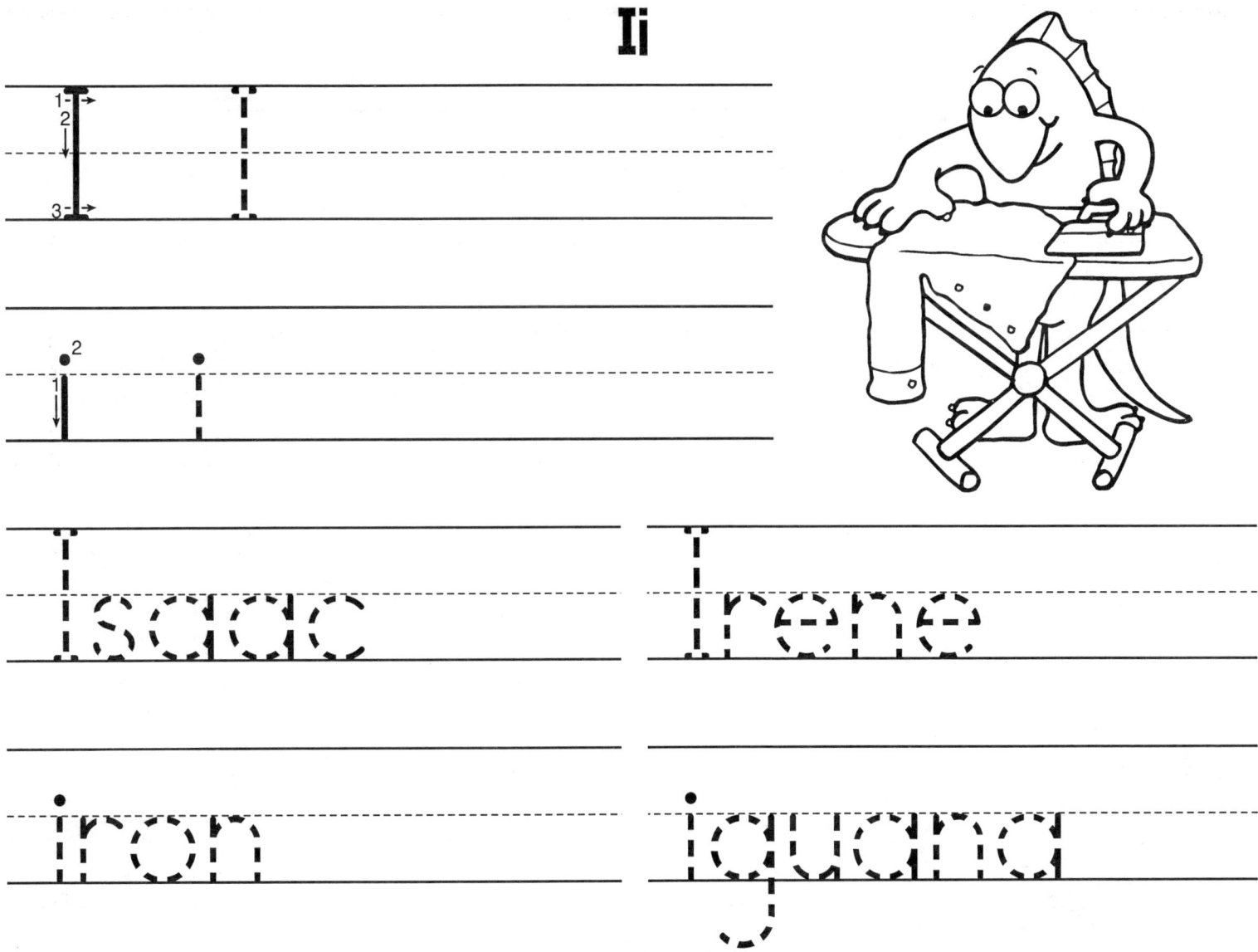

Jj

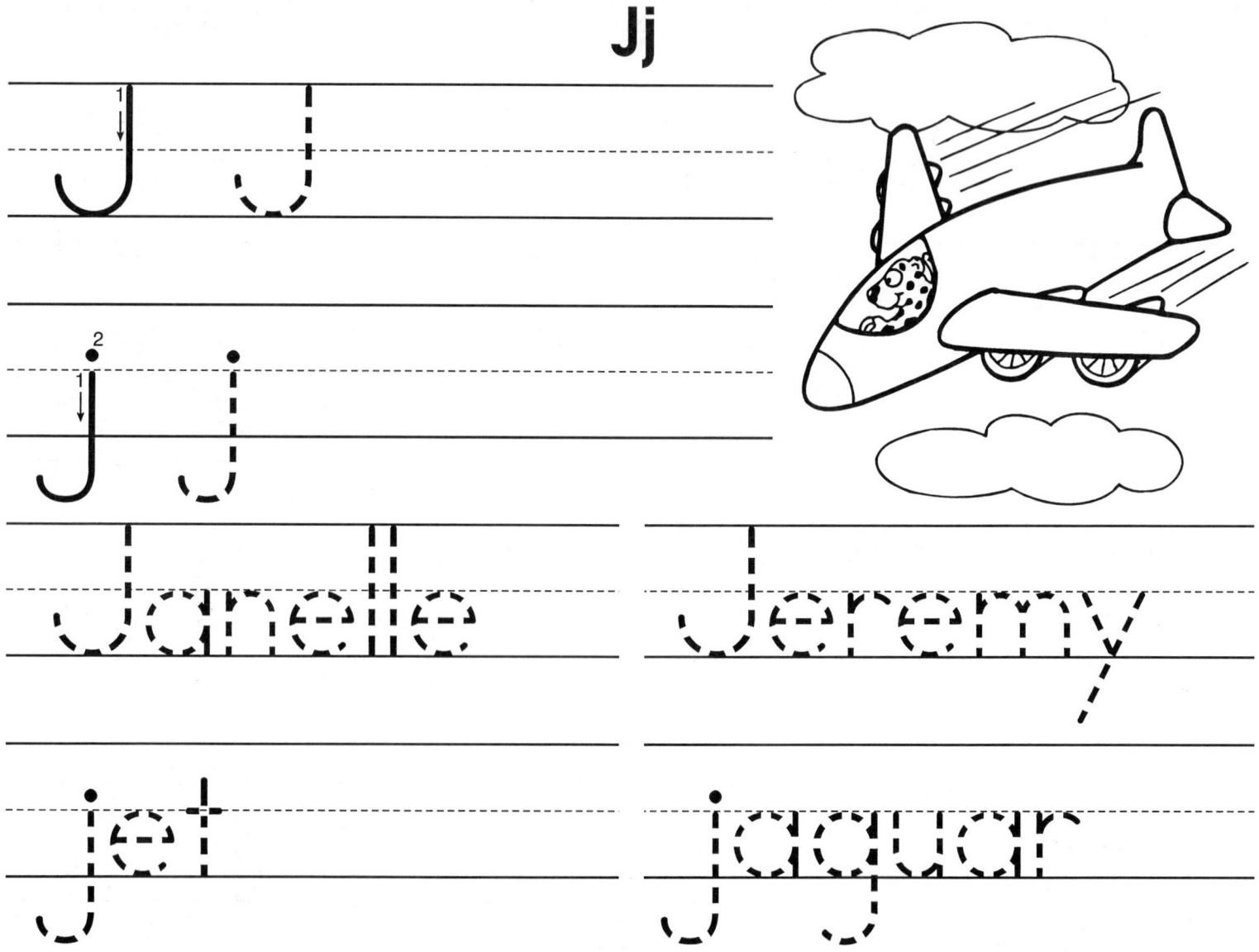

Kk

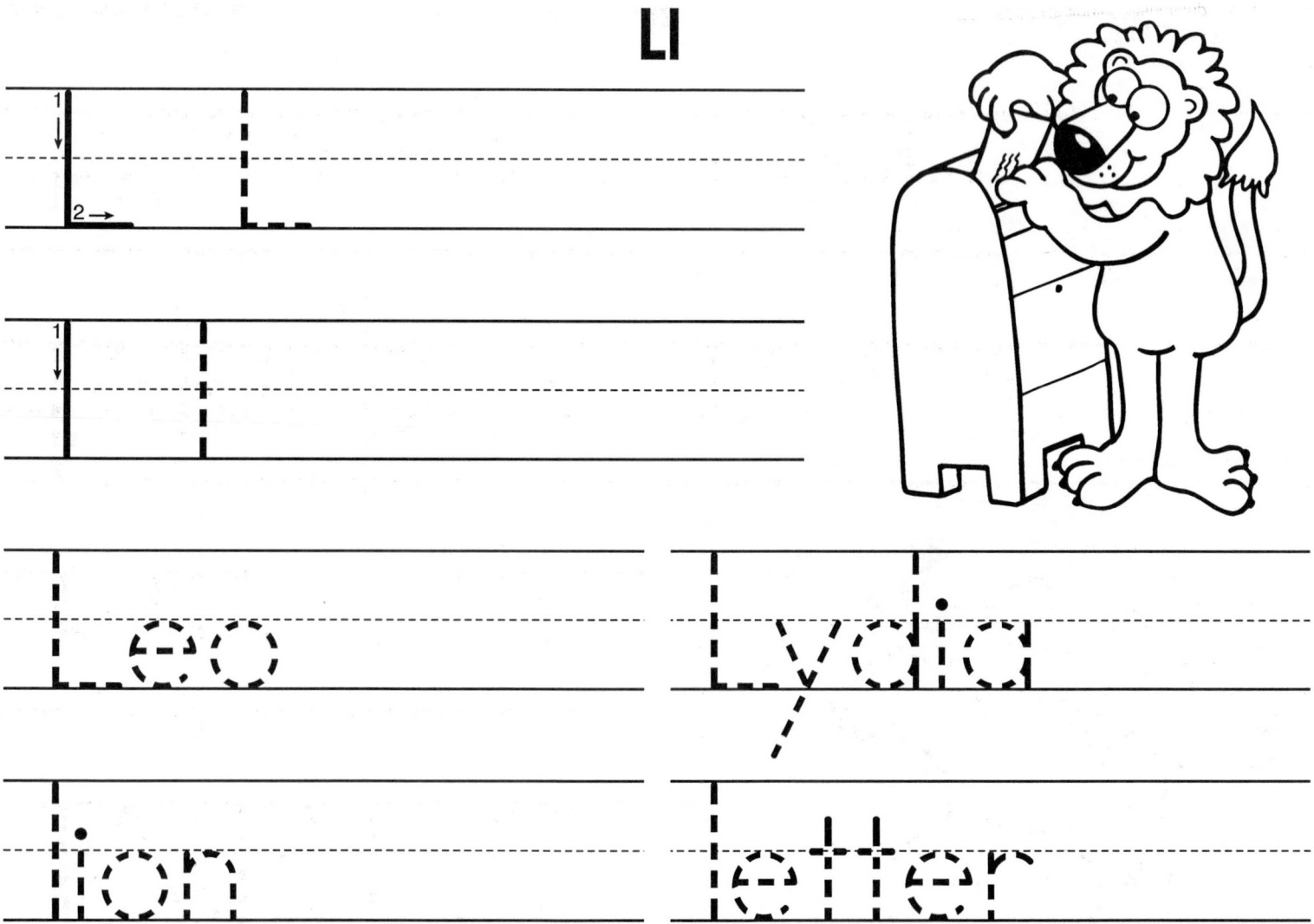

Mm

Mm

mm

Marco   Mimi

monkey   map

13

Nn

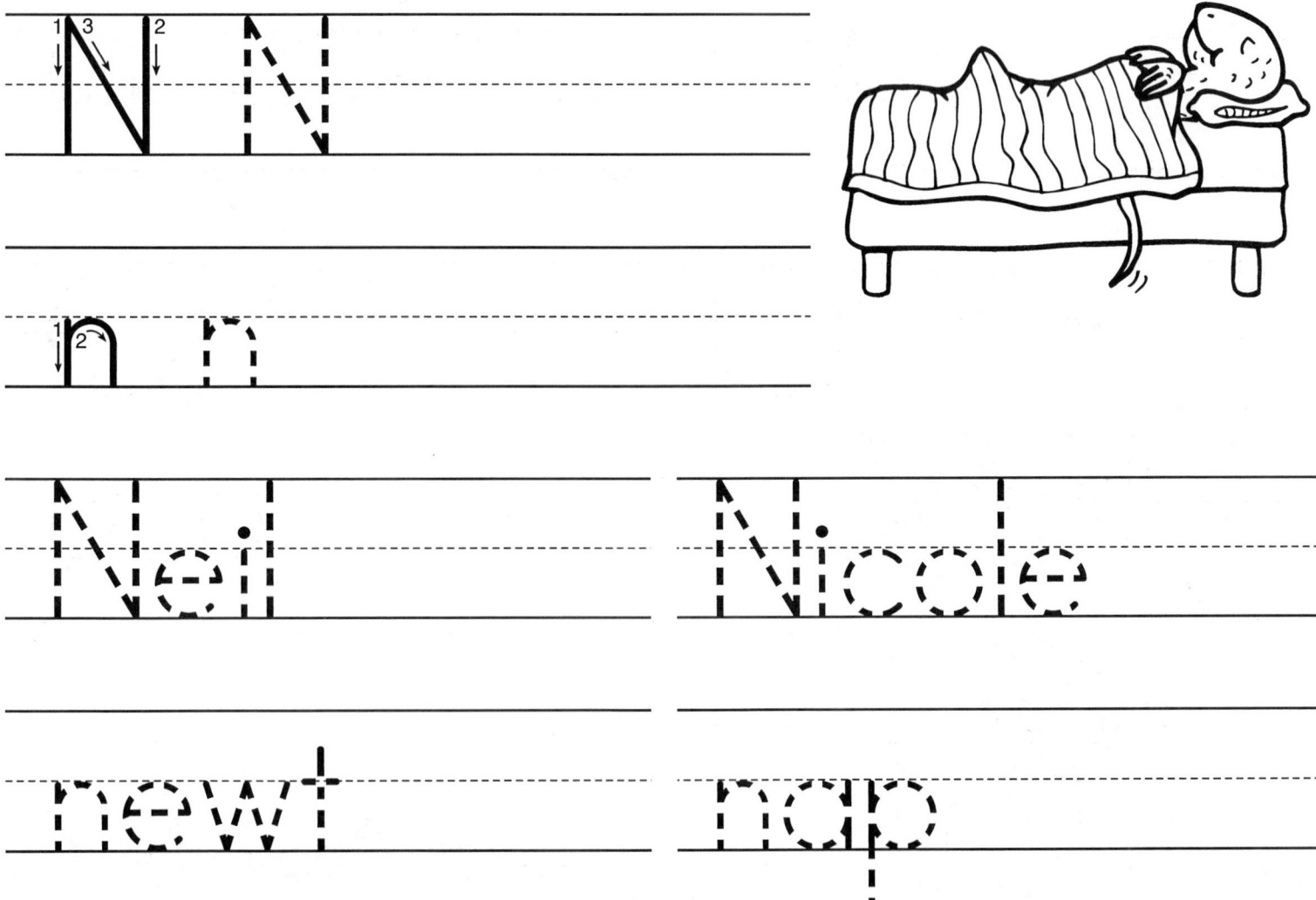

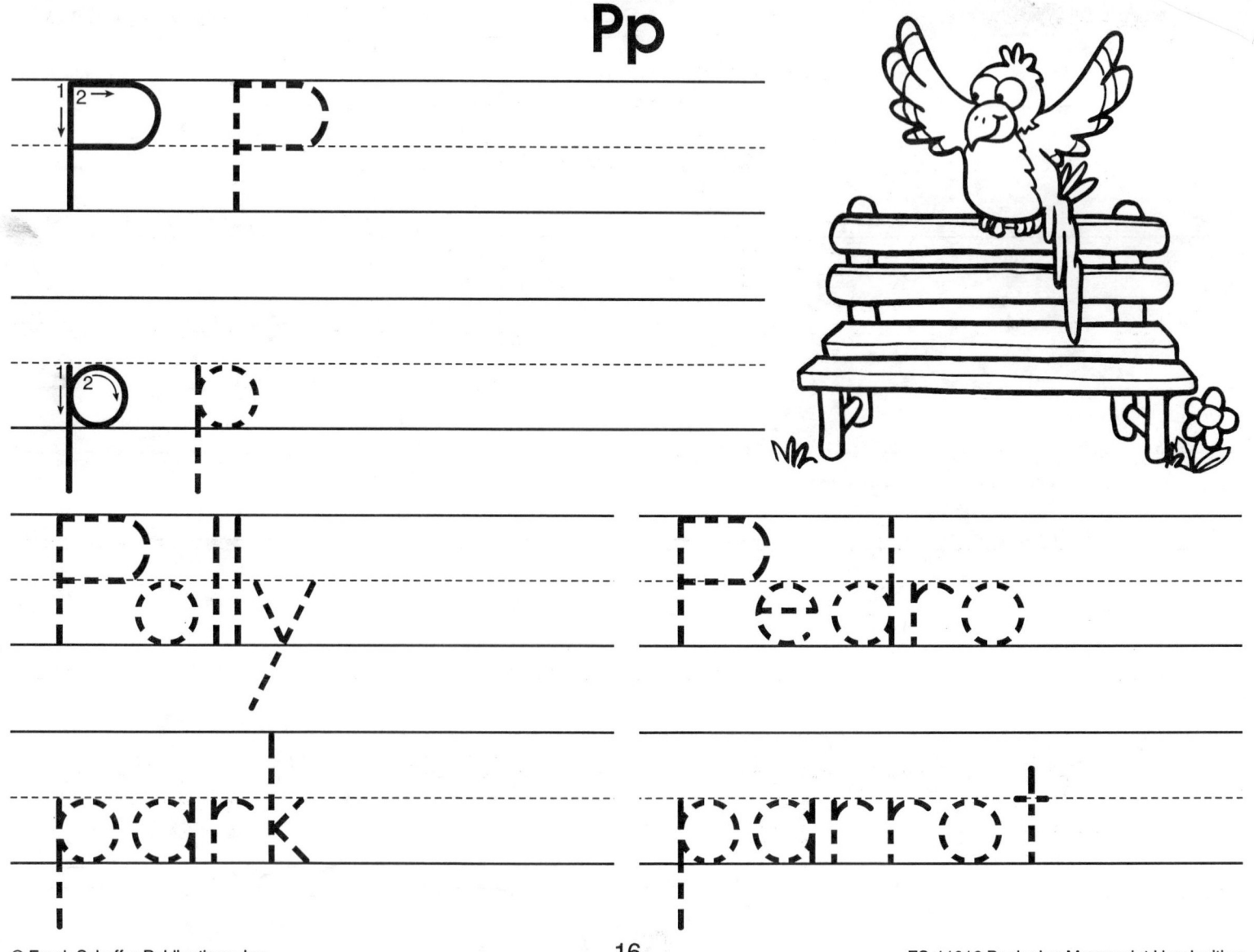

Rr

Ss

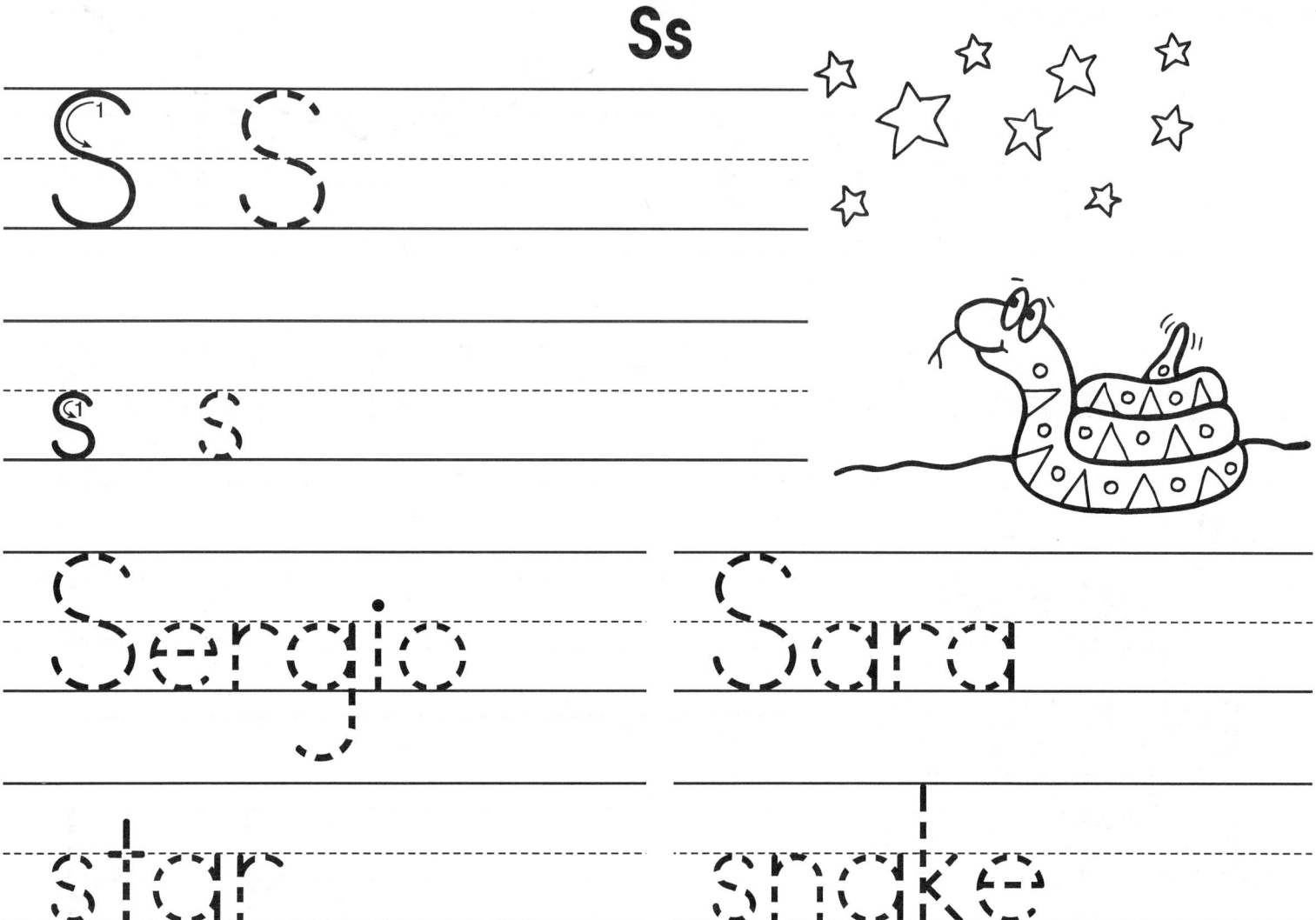

S S

s s

Sergio Sara

star snake

Uu

U U

u u

Ursula   Ulysses

umbrella   unicorn

Vv

Ww

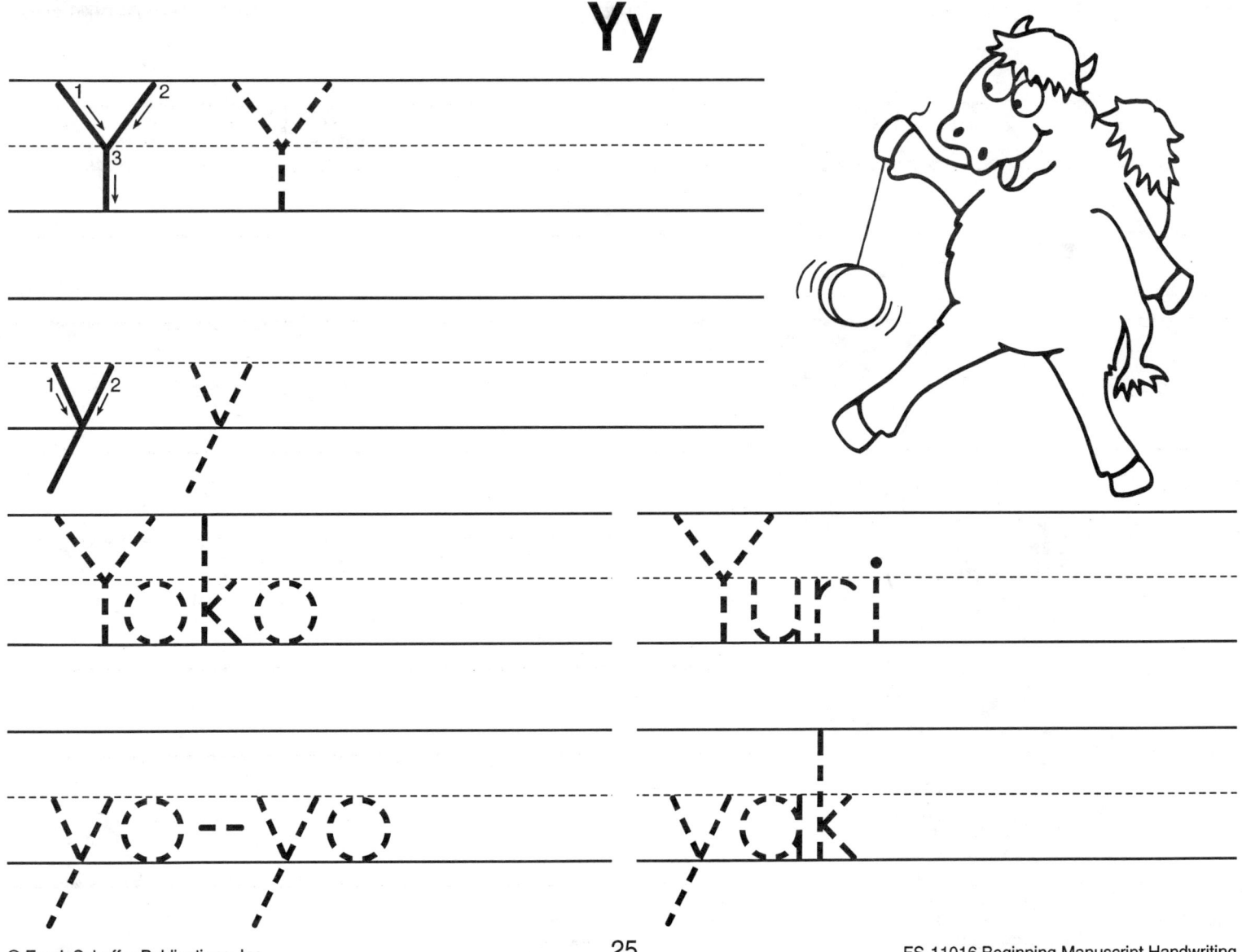

Zz

Zz

Zz

Zoe   Zane

zipper   zebra

26

Aa

Aaron ate apples.

Aaron ate apples.

Bb

Busy bees buzz.

Busy bees buzz.

Cc

Cats cut cakes.

Catscutcakes.

Dd

Ducks dive deep.

Ducksdivedeep.

Ee

Erin eats eggs.

Ff

Five foxes fish.

Gg

Goats go golfing.

33

Hh

Hens have hats.

Ii

Is Ivan in Italy?

Jj

Jim juggles jars.

Kk

Kangaroos kick.

Ll

Lila laughs loudly.

Mm

Meg mixes mud.

Nn

Nina nibbles nuts.

Oo

Otto owns oboes.

Pp

Paul picks poppies.

Qq

Queens quilt quickly.

Rr

Rats run races.

Ss

Sue sips soup.

Tt

Two turtles tiptoe.

Uu

Umpires unite.

Vv

Violet visits Vern.

Ww

Wanda worries.

Xx

Xavier x-rays x's.

Yy

Yvette yawns.

Zz

Zach zips zippers.

Numbers 0–3

53

Numbers 4–7

Numbers 8-10

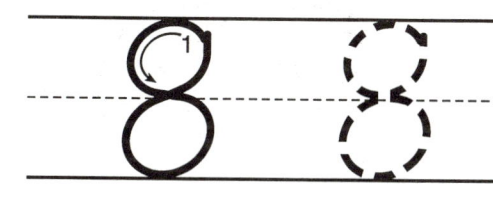

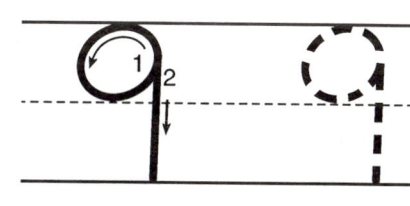

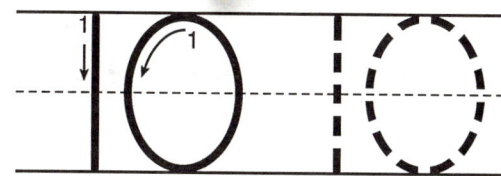

Write your phone number below.

What's My Name?

Write your first and last names in your very best handwriting.